THE
PERFECT
DIALOGUE

Master The Art Of Talking To Your Partner

Rachel Carpenter

Table of Contents

Chapter 1:

7 Ways To Achieve Harmony In Personal Relationships

How beautiful the world or life would be if we were all blessed with harmonious relationships. The kind that is selfless, giving, and nurturing, the kind that doesn't have any tussle of egos and power play. Just you and your significant other fitted together, like a hand in the glove. Harmony isn't an inherent trait; that is one of the reasons why it becomes too difficult for relationships to flow seamlessly. Here are some tips and tricks to build a harmonious relationship with others.

1. Harmony Can Be Nurtured

Before getting into the ways to let go of all the negativities and build a holistic, harmonious relationship, we must first understand why harmonious relationships are essential. A harmonious person is defined as someone who is easygoing and has the ability to get along well with others. A harmonious bond is something that two people experience without fighting, clashes, or ego tussles. But most of the time, one of the partners might feel negative emotions, which can affect the quality of the relationship. Feeling discontent in a relationship might have distressing and overwhelming experiences, but that does not in any way means that we should lose all hope.

2. Be the best version of yourself:

If you look into your personal relationships to compensate for your loneliness, you are bound to get disappointed sooner or later. It indeed takes two to tango, but building a relationship and making sure it lasts has a lot to do with your state of mind. You have to be peaceful with yourself first before achieving peace in your personal relationships. Over-expecting things from your partners or others would always lead to disappointment, which will, in turn, channel into challenges and difficulties in your relationship. You have to be the bearer of harmony that you wish to cultivate in your relationships. You can start by fixing the broken things on your end, and others will eventually follow you.

3. Embrace acceptance:

Resistance and harmony can never go hand in hand. If you wish to achieve harmony, you have to let go of resisting the current order of things or change. Resistance can be in the form of criticizing your partner for whatever behaviors and traits they possess and forcing them to change who they are. This would lead to negativity and tension in the relationship. Going from resistance to acceptance is a passable road that will lead you towards building a harmonious relationship. You have to be aware that no one is perfect, even ourselves. We are bound to make mistakes and have flaws and have to accept others and their defects and errors.

4. Let go of the hurt and negativity:

Sometimes, it's our baggage of the past that keeps us unable to build a harmonious relationship. For example, it might be something that your ex-partner did to immensely hurt you, or a family member criticized you. However, you didn't process this hurt nor gave it the time to heal, but instead decided to bottle up your decisions and move on. It is only natural that the negative feelings you are keeping inside you for a long time will come out when someone bad triggers you. In this case, you have to find a way to let go of whatever hurt you're feeling, channel all your negativity, and foster harmony in your relationships.

5. Practice compassion:

You have to internalize gentleness and compassion, both as an individual and a couple if you want to build a close and harmonious relationship. When you address and approach any conflict and issue with gentleness, your mind will automatically respond with empathy rather than jumping to conclusions. This will facilitate open communication and inhibitions. It will also enable you to view the other person's perspective and views with kindness. This would put you in a position to give your partner space to process their thoughts and emotions.

6. Free yourself from expectations:

The stringent expectations we might feel from our loved ones can take a toll on our equation with them. While it is only natural to expect some things from the people we love, we shouldn't set them in stone. Because unmet expectations lead to a handful of negative emotions of disappointment, hurt, and anger, you end up saying hurtful things to other people. Instead of expecting too much, accept them as they are, allow them to be their own person, and appreciate the good they bring into the relationship. Appreciate their efforts even if they don't go your way.

7. Give and seek space in your relationships:

Personal space is one of the rarest yet one of the most crucial elements of feeling at peace in your relationships. Oftentimes, we get so much tethered with our loved ones that it feels like a permanent embrace. It may seem exciting and comforting at first, but soon it will leave you guys feeling suffocated from each other. We must understand that everyone needs their space t catch a breath, reflect, unwind and grow. It is also a hallmark of a healthy bond. To build a harmonious relationship, you must dismantle the clingy approach and give each other all the space you need.

Conclusion:

A harmonious relationship needs sustained efforts and nurturing, and you can neither expect to achieve harmony overnight nor do expect it to last forever once achieved. But it is sure is worth every effort. The importance of building a harmonious relationship lies in the fact that it brings you peace and hope, the two things most vital to any individual.

Chapter 2:

5 Languages of Love

What is that one element that fills the human heart with great colors? That is love. The essential factors in our life that make us grow as an individual as well as in pairs. No matter where you stand in your life, there is always this one element somehow involved within you. That is human nature to love. The five languages of love are the different ways to express love. People may have their way of loving others, but they will still fall in one of these five categories. Gary Chapman developed these five languages of love in one of his famous books, "The five love languages: the secret to love that lasts."

The essential part of a relationship is communication. Without it, love is incomplete. Gary Chapman made our lives easier by introducing these five ways to show and receive love. He showed us the way towards everlasting love. It teaches us that understanding each other and communicating are the keys to one's heart. It brings in the romantic feeling that one adores. What else would anyone else want? These are the five languages that grow us.

1. Words Of Encouragement

We would love to hear sweet and affirmative things all day long. And it's one of the most romantic ways to describe your feelings through words. In a relationship, words mean a lot. Those small "I love you" and "you make me happy" make butterflies flutter in our stomachs. It's no surprise that one may fall in love with you because of this language of love. It's the short and simple formula to keep your other half happy and satisfied. They will always feel comfortable in your words and will give you some of their own. That is why it is said that "choose your words wisely."

2. Standard Hours

When your partner wants to spend time with you, it's evident that you will feel adored. Spending quality time with each other is the best way to grow together and bond with each other. It's essential to be there for each other in times of need to feel loved and cared about. It would help if you made them feel your presence. Make eye contact with them. Hold them. They will feel safe and comfortable. Let them know you are there for them. Spend quality time with them any chance you get.

3. Acts Of Service

People who think that action speaks louder than words can do acts of service for their partners. Showing little acts of affection like taking care of them is the most romantic feeling ever. They took care of them when they were sick, held them when they needed to, and made coffee for them in the morning. These little actions speak loud. Your partner will feel pampered with this. This love language is all about showing compassion towards each other. Taking care is a type of love language itself. These acts of service go straight to each other's hearts.

4. Physical Touch

Physical affection is one of the love languages that makes a relationship much better. Physical touch doesn't necessarily mean sex, but holding each other's hands, hugging each other when needed, and holding each other. These slight physical affection can make a person feel loved and admired by their partner. This way, you can show just how much you need each other's physical presence in each other's life. It's the intelligent formula to let your corresponding others know that you will always be there for them. Physical touch is as romantic as any other language of love, sometimes even more.

5. Giving and Receiving Presents

Who doesn't want gifts and presents from their partners? Of course, we all do. Giving a personalized present speaks the language of love. Something your partners have wanted for a long time, and you give them that as a gift. That moment of happiness will be worth it.

On the other hand, receiving such kind of treatment is wondrous. When your other half remembers all about your choices and likes and gives you something. You feel loved. It's a love language that is personalized and pampered with passion and love. It would help if you made each other feel as if you know them better even than themselves.

Conclusion

These five languages of love make relationships everlasting. When you take care of each other's needs and priorities, your partner will automatically fall in love with you. These are the ways you can make someone your lifelong partner and love them forever.

Chapter 3:

Make Time for Your Partner

When I first got into my relationship, I thought my boyfriend and my 100-hour workweek would have to battle it out until the bitter end. Yet somehow, I've managed to maintain both. It turns out there are a lot of weird ways to make time for your partner when you're busy AF. You may have to get creative and resort to some weird measures, but I am living proof that there is no such thing as being too busy for your loved ones.

We all have to run errands. That time is gone from your workday anyway. So, why not use it to show your partner you care instead of just getting what you need? Picking up each other's shampoo and favorite cereal (or, perhaps more practically, take turns picking up groceries and toiletries for the both of you) is one way to connect without needing to make any more time in your schedule.

You spend the same amount of time cooking for two people as you do for one, but since you're feeding two, you *save* time by doing this. Think about it: Instead of cooking every night, you only have to do it every *other* night. Even if you both eat it in front of your computers, making food for each other is a loving gesture that'll make you appreciate each other.

If you live together, you'll probably be sleeping in the same bed anyway. But even if you don't, your dates can consist solely of sleeping if that's what it takes to make time for each other. Or, if you can't sleep through the night with someone else next to you, you can try just sharing nap time.

Even if you don't get around to working out that much, the time you can devote to exercise will help clear your mind, so it's worthwhile if you can make it out for a short run or yoga class. Plus, working out together can boost your attraction by releasing endorphins.

I can't always handle this, especially when I need to feel like nobody wants my attention to focus. But for less intensive tasks, it can be comforting to cuddle up to your significant other while you're working. You can even be each other's sounding boards if you need help coming up with ideas.

This one will not work for everyone. But if you have an office in a similar place, your walk or ride to work can be your bonding time, even if it's just part of the way. Even just a shared walk to the train station can pay off if you think ahead enough to coordinate your trips to and from work.

Chapter 4:

9 New Date Ideas That Will Deepen Your Relationship

When you commit to a relationship, you need to know your partner well. If you don't know your partner, then how do you expect your relationship to last? A date is something that someone plans for their partner. Dates usually involve doing something or going somewhere with your partner, and you find it fun, but sometimes everybody gets bored of the same cliché date ideas. Sometimes, these kinds of dates aren't enough to know your partner. Surely you want to deepen your bond with your partner. Here are some new date ideas to deepen your relationship.

1. Go For A Walk

We have often seen people go for a walk to clear their minds. Walking helps people think differently. It is not exactly an epic date idea, but it will remove both of your brains. It'll help you talk to each other. When you and your partner start talking more, your bond will automatically deepen. After the walk, you will feel very fresh, but you will also feel like you now know your partner more.

2. Read A Book Together

As a kid, we all loved to hear some bedtime stories, but we forgot how blissful it felt as we grew up. At night when both of you feel tired, then select a book you both like, lay down and read it to each other in turns.

3. Spa At Home

We all need some time to relax. You don't always have to go outside for a date, and you could give yourself a day off and bring out all the face, hair, and every other mask you have because this is a spa day, you could give each other massages and help the other relax. Also, don't forget the scented candles.

4. Plan Trips Together

Haven't we all dreamed about discovering the world but don't tell anyone, well what are you waiting for? Sit together and look through places you would want to visit even if you can't right now! Daydreaming isn't a sin.

5. Go For A Boat Ride

Have you watched tangled? If yes, you would surely want to experience that romantic scene on the boat; if you haven't still done it, what are you waiting for? Rent a boat, take your partner with you. It'll just be you, your partner, and the stars. You could set some slow music on your phone and enjoy that quality time with your partner.

6. Take A Step Out Of Your Comfort Zone

Almost all of us have a fixed routine, but it is good to mess with your way once in a while. As a couple, you would have a place where you usually go for food, a cinema where you typically watch a movie, an ice cream parlor where you usually buy the ice cream from but isn't it all getting boring? This is the time to forget about your comfort zone and explore something else. Go to a new restaurant, a museum you haven't been to before together, or any other place you and your partner haven't visited yet.

7. Paint Together

Not all of us are good at painting, but what's stopping you from painting something together. It sounds fun, doesn't it? Just buy a few art supplies and a canvas and paint whatever you want to paint. Then hang it somewhere; it seems nice, it doesn't need to be an artistic masterpiece, but it'll bring back the memories of that fantastic day whenever you look at it.

8. Watch The Sunset Together

There are many places where you can see the sunset together, so find the home that feels perfect to you and take your partner there for a date and watch the sunset together along with your partner's favorite dish to eat. Not only will this bring a wide smile to your partner's face, but it'll also help you deepen your connection with them.

9. Meet At A Coffee Shop

At the start of a relationship, most people decide to meet at a coffee shop, but as time passes, they don't do it anymore, but why not? Decide a time and a coffee shop and meet up there. Drink coffee and eat something if you like. You will have fun with this typical date idea.

Conclusion:

These simple and fun ideas will help you deepen your relationship with your partner. Don't fret if you think you don't know your partner much because it is never too late. Just put in some effort, and your bond with your partner would be more profound than the ocean.

Chapter 5:

<u>7 Habits of Healthy Relationships</u>

Relationships are the social strings that hold us together. We are tied to our loved ones by relationships. Sadly, we also regret being linked, by our relationships, to people of questionable character. There are those relationships we are in by default and others by design – meaning we are in them in our free will, without any coercion whatsoever.

Here are 7 habits of healthy relationships:

1. <u>Making It Symbiotic</u>

It is a selfish foundation but it is what relationships truly are. Healthy relationships are symbiotic between the partners. Both parties benefit from its existence. They are equal partners and bring something to the table.

When partners in a relationship have a mutual interest in a course, they will work towards achieving it. They understand that any failure is a loss to all of them. This is a powerful drive to make them work towards staying united because they need each other.

Symbiosis is the mechanism of adaptation to nature. The relationship between bees and flowers is an example of a healthy relationship. The bees depend on nectar from flowers to make food while flowers depend on bees to be agents of cross-pollination. It is a win-win for both of them.

2. Pursuing A Common Goal

Two heads are better than one. When people are united by a course they believe in, the relationship is stronger and healthier. There is a reason more than their selfish interests that brings them together.

The promise of success by achieving this common goal makes the relationship healthy – devoid of any backstabbing from either party. As long as partners in a relationship have a common objective, nothing can come between them.

If you have a relationship you want to salvage, find a common ground to stand on. This will give you more reason not to give up on the relationship. Consider the relationship between a man and his fiancé. What is common between them is love and the desire to start a family together. Challenges will come their way but whatever holds them together is greater than what divides them. In the end, love wins.

3. They Are Not Exclusive

Some relationships, especially romantic ones, tend to be exclusive to two people. The two people give themselves to each other completely, withholding nothing. Any foreign person that comes between them is considered hostile and unwanted.

However, healthy relationships are not exclusive. They give room to the third voice of reason which will whisper some advice or rebuke some ills they do. The view of a third eye is golden. It will see what the two of you overlook. The simple, repetitive, toxic habits that bring down relationships will not thrive in yours because you have allowed an experienced eye to be the guardian angel.

This is not to imply that there should be no privacy. Privacy is beautiful in relationships. It only stops being one when it overrides your well-being and stops your relationship from budding.

4. It Happens Naturally

Murphy's law states that *anything that can go wrong will go wrong.* Relationships are not exceptional either. Regardless of how many times you try to resuscitate a dying relationship, if it can go wrong then it will go wrong.

Healthy relationships are those that happen automatically. There is no within or external force that works on making them stick. There is a special vibe from those in the relationship. They bond naturally. Partners in automatic relationships do not struggle to be together, it is as if nature herself has blessed them 'to be fruitful and multiply.'

In automatic relationships, you do not ignore the red flags. This kind is not blind. When you see red flags in your relationships and continue living in denial, murphy's law will apply. Settle down to re-evaluate; is it that your spouse is too perfect, or are you ignoring the red alerts all over?

5. Balanced Selfishness

What a vice for healthy relationships to thrive in! They are selfish enough to put their interests above those of everyone else. Do not judge; it is completely natural in this world of survival for the fittest. Most importantly is that those in relationships act as a unit. They are not selfish to each other but to the rest of the world.

This vice waters the success of relationships. Not everyone has your best interests at heart. Some will try to infiltrate your relationship and cause havoc. Beware of such people. It is the reason why relationships must be selfish.

Consider the example of bees. They jealously and viciously guard their queen and the honey they make. They are selfish with it and their safety is non-negotiable. Even bee farmers have to wear protective clothing when they want to harvest honey. Their selfishness is what unites them, how beautiful!

6. Making Investments

Investment is a sign of trust. You invest in someone or something you have confidence in. Partners in healthy relationships invest in each other because they trust in each other. The best foundation of healthy relationships is trust because in it, you can be yourself.

Why should you be in a relationship with someone you cannot trust? The fact that you cannot be yourself with your partner is sufficient not to be involved with them.

You invest in relationships because you are assured of returns. The safest place to be is in a fulfilling one. Healthy relationships go far because their partners invest their time and resources in them.

7. Clearly Marked Boundaries

Regions and territories are demarcated by boundaries. They partition countries, provinces, and estates. So important are they that border disputes are treated with utmost seriousness anywhere in the world. The latest border dispute in East Africa being the unresolved maritime dispute between Kenya and Somalia.

Likewise, healthy relationships have boundaries. The partners are mature enough not to suffocate each other. It is paramount that in a relationship, for example, between a man and his fiancée, that they allow each other space to live their lives.

Healthy relationships are not suffocating or dominating. There is a boundary that those in relationships do not cross. If not for anything else, it is for peace to prevail. It does not mean that trust is lacking in the relationship. On the contrary, it signals that you trust your partner enough not to betray whatever relationship you share.

These 7 habits are paramount for healthy relationships. When you religiously observe them, you will have a testimony of a turning point in your relationships.

Chapter 6:

6 Ways To Make Your Relationship Sweeter

Being in love is the most beautiful thing ever for some of us. Everything seems bright and colorful. You feel happy all the time, and the things you once hated seem good enough to try. However, everything takes time. When you both grow together and get to know each other better, it takes a lot of time. And of course, having strong feelings for each other is necessary for a relationship. A relationship is a way of loving someone openly and keeping someone your priority by your own free will and being someone else's priority too.

Relationships are sweet on their own. There is not much hard work needed when you are naturally and effortlessly in love with each other. Even though there are countless ways, you can dial a notch up and make your relationship even more robust, healthier, and sweeter than before. It takes a lot of time to manage everything, but love is worth it when you are with the right person. All the work and compromises seem worth it. Once you are with your charming prince and your dream princess, everything other than that is just a piece of cake. Following are some ways to make your relationship even sweeter.

1. **Go On A date Occasionally**

Going on a date with the one that you love is highly romantic and sweet. It's essential to keep that spark alive between the two of you, and a date might be a perfect idea to spend some time together. It is not necessary to go out every time. Cuddling and movies sound like a sweet and comfortable date. It's easier for you to tire out of all the work of the day. A date might give you that energy boost that you need. No matter how long you have been dating, a date is perfect for you.

2. **Share Your Day**

Going through a hectic schedule is much work on themselves. When we come home to someone who will listen to us rant about every detail of our hectic day, our day gets better somehow. We get a weird sense of comfort to know that there might be someone willing to listen to us every day. The same goes the other way around; you need to listen attentively and remember the details. This shows that you care about your partner and your relationship turns sweeter.

3. **Complement Each Other**

When you try to look your best, put on your best dress and do on-point make-up. All you need is someone to compliment you on putting that charming smile on your face too. In a relationship, when both people compliment each other, not only does it sound sweet, but it boosts the confidence of the other partner. It would be best to remind your other half that they look perfect no matter how they dress or look because it's the love that matters.

4.   Constant "I love you's."

When you randomly tell your partner how much you love them, nothing can be much sweeter than that. Those small moments of saying "I love you" can mean a lot to the other person. It might make their difficult day brighter. It can make them lose all their stress in an instant—elaborate your love. Tell them why you love them. Tell them you make them happy. It makes a relationship much more robust than before.

5.   Physical Affection

Showing physical affection to each other sounds so romantic, as romantic as it feels. You were looking into each other's eyes, holding each other's hand and cuddling with each other. These small gestures may sound bland and ordinary. But they can feel like you have conquered the world. These are the feelings that make a bond more assertive and make a relationship sweeter. It would be best if you kept the flirting moving on to keep the spark alive in your relationship.

6.   Gifts and Presents

You don't need a special occasion to gift your partner something. Surprise them randomly. It doesn't mean expensive gifts or unaffordable presents. Something sweet and personal will make them happy too. Like making their favorite dish or dessert, buying them their favorite perfume, or gift them something that personally means a lot to both of you. These simple ideas can make their whole day special.

Conclusion:

Maintaining a relationship might not be as easy as it sounds, but when you are with the one you live and love to spend time with, then everything can be bearable. You need to keep the spark alive and keep each other strong individually as well.

Chapter 7:

5 Ways To Communicate Your Emotional Needs

It's not as easy as it sounds. It's far more challenging to communicate your emotional needs. Especially when you are considered an introvert and are always thinking about others, others always push us back, and we constantly believe not to disappoint or burden them with our emotional needs and wants. That thinking of pleasing others always ends as our loss. Mentally as well as emotionally. One major step towards identifying your goal would be the path of understanding your own emotions first. If you are confused about your feelings, it will be more challenging to reflect them in your actions.

Vulnerability and self-reflection are the main factors to point out your emotions, and that way, it will be easier to show others what you feel. Self-communication is very important in this regard. Think about what you need. Forget about society, family, and friends for a while and start thinking only about what you need or want. Please make sure they are your thoughts without any brainwashing from the outsiders. This way, we will get aware of our own personal and emotional needs. Here are some easier ways to communicate your moving needs.

1. Privacy

A person needs to be wise with their words. Make sure you keep things to yourself as much as possible. It doesn't mean to stay away from people. Right things at appropriate times matter. Keep your point firmly and try not to explain it again and again. Reflect your emotion in your sentence. Make sure others get aware of your feelings just by the way you are talking. Keep things to yourself that are not necessary to discuss with others. Talk with people, be a little outgoing too. The main point is to be careful.

2. Be Confident

You need to make sure that others know what you need. Confidently put up to them. Be rightfully confident to have your needs. Confidence is critical while communicating with someone. People will listen attentively when they know you won't waste their time while being shy and difficult. It would be best if you practiced confidence. It won't come naturally but with time and work. But people will acknowledge your emotional needs when you are confident about them.

3. Observation

People who keep to themselves mostly tend to have an on-point observation about things. If you constantly look at your phone, they will notice that without any unique analysis. When you observe something about someone that disturbs you or affects you mentally somehow, you need to point it out. You need to get that observation in their knowledge so they would know what they are doing wrong. Keeping it to yourself will disturb you even more, and this will continue until they get aware of it any other way. There is possibly less chance that someone else would tell them. So, you have to do it yourself. Take your courage, tell them whatever you think is right. That is a way to communicate your emotional needs to others.

4. Don't Hold The Issues For Too Long

Any issue that occurs in your life needs to be addressed. But if someone is ignorant about it, you need not make them listen again and again. Stop over-explaining. Keep your issue on the table once or twice. If you observe that the other person doesn't get it, then let that issue go entirely. This will save you emotional energy and lots of time. People who care about you will listen to you the first time you complain about something. They would ant to work pon that if not, there is nothing more someone can do.

5. Be Open-Minded

Don't close yourself to the world. When something you want needs to be put out there, then be open-minded about it. No matter if it's your relationship, your friendship, or any other association. It would be best if you were open about your emotional needs. Communicate with them so they will know your needs better. If something bothers you, ask questions about it without hesitation. They will take your hesitation as the poor choice of decision when it's just your mind trying to let it go. But that would be against our emotional needs.

Conclusion:

We all have our emotional needs and wants. What we need is a way to communicate it with other people. We need to make sure they know how stressful they can get by being ignorant about our needs. Communication is the key to any relationship. Communicating your emotional needs is just as important.

Chapter 8:

Happy People Engage in Deep Meaningful Conversations

Psychologist Matthias Mehl and his team set out to study happiness and deep talk. In the journal Psychological Science, his study involved college students who wore an electronically activated recorder with a microphone on their shirt collar that captured 30-second snippets of conversation every 12.5 minutes for four days. Effectively, this created a conversational "diary" of their day.

Then researchers went through the conversations and categorized them as either small talk (talk about the weather, a recent TV show, etc.) or more substantive discussion (talk about philosophy, current affairs, etc.). Researchers were careful not to automatically label specific topics a certain way—if the speakers analyzed a TV show's characters and their motivations, this conversation was considered substantive.

The researchers found that about a third of the students' conversations were considered substantive, while a fifth consisted of small talk. Some conversations didn't fit neatly into either category, such as discussions that focused on practical matters like who would take out the trash.

The researchers also studied how happy the participants were, drawing data from life satisfaction reports the students completed and feedback from people in their lives.

The results? Mehl and his team found that the happiest person in the study had twice as many substantive conversations, and only one-third the small talk, as the unhappiest person. Almost every other conversation the happiest person had—about 46 percent of the day's conversations—was substantive.

As for the unhappiest person, only 22 percent of that individual's conversations were substantive, while small talk made up only 10 percent of the happiest person's conversations.

Does small talk equal unhappiness? Score one for Team Introvert because we've known this all along.

How to Have More Meaningful Conversations

instead of

- "How are you?"

- "How was your weekend?"

- "Where did you grow up?"

- "What do you do for a living?"

Try

- "What's your story?"

- "What was your favorite part of your weekend?"

- "Tell me something interesting about where you grew up."

- "What drew you to your line of work?"

Why Is Happiness Linked with Deep Talk?

Further research is still needed because it's not clear whether people make themselves happier by having substantive conversations or whether people who are already happy choose to engage in meaningful talk. However, one thing is evident: Happiness and meaningful interactions go hand-in-hand.

In an interview with the *New York Times*, Mehl discussed the reasons he thinks substantive conversations are linked to happiness. For one, humans are driven to create meaning in their lives, and substantive conversations help us do that, he said. Also, human beings—both introverts and extroverts—are social animals who have a real need to connect with others. Substantive conversation connects, while small talk doesn't.

Chapter 9:
How Not To Control Everything

Steve Maraboli once said, "You must learn to let go. Release the stress. You were never in control anyway." Now, it goes without saying that things flow much more smoothly when you give up control when you let them be natural when you allow them to happen instead of making them happen. Being a control freak can drain so much of your mental energy without you even knowing it. It can cause you to fall into a never-ending loop of overthinking. We obsess over controlling every aspect of life without realizing the negative effects it can cause to our health, goals, and relationships. We grab them so tightly until we suffocate and kill them eventually.

Mastering the art of letting go and not controlling everything is not easy, but we should trust our instincts and know that it will be okay no matter the circumstances. We should always open ourselves to opportunities and possibilities. The path that we control and attach ourselves desperately to isn't always the right one. There would be other valuable and productive paths if we naturally and smoothly sail onto them. Letting go of control means more freedom, peace, joy, support, and connection. It will be hard at first, but once you get your hands on it, it'll become easier and easier for you.

The first and foremost thing to do is to use your imagination. We often find ourselves overthinking the worst possibilities that could happen to us. It's like using all of your energy, time and head on climbing the steepest mountain when you can take the stairs easily and free yourself from all the stress. So, the next time you find yourself in a controlling mindset, think of all the emotional and physical energy that you might drain in trying to control a simple situation. Embrace the freedom of not having to climb that mountain and just let go and wait for whatever it is that's going to happen.

Control is usually rooted in fear. But, understand that fear is merely an illusion, its false evidence may appear real, but it's very much fake. We control things because we fear what might happen if we don't. We attach ourselves to expectations and then set ourselves up for disappointment. So, focus on grounding yourself. Take a walk in the park, meditate, relax your mind. The positive energy will only flow in when the negative energy flows out.

Have a firm belief in yourself and practice saying affirmations. Deduct any self doubts that you have and keep reassuring yourself. Recognize the importance of freedom and see what it means to you. Once you start enjoying your space, the act of controlling everything will begin to annoy you.

Change your views about life. Could you work with your life, not against it? The sooner you realize that life is beautiful and on your side, the easier it will be for you not to control everything. You would be open to opportunities and would accept whatever it will give you. If life is moving you in one direction, instead of wasting your energy in resisting and fighting it, embrace it and work towards its betterment. Some things are beyond our control; only control what you can and let go of what you cannot.

Chapter 10:

6 Gestures That Make People Feel Loved

"Actions speak louder than words ', this phrase is commonly used around us, but hardly anyone knows the real meaning of this phrase. This phrase tells us something about love and the importance of a person. Our actions define us. These actions affect the people around us, it speaks to them in words, we can't speak in. Loving someone is not just enough. You need to show your love, and sometimes the smallest of gestures can make you feel more loved than ever. Everyone wants to feel loved and cared about, and if you truly love them, then show your love, even if it is through a straightforward small text saying, "I miss you." Here are a few ways to make people feel loved.

1. **Write Them Notes**

Waking up to a heartwarming note on your bedside tables makes someone's day. So whenever you want to show someone how much you love them, just leave them a letter or card. It doesn't matter if you write a few words, either thanking them or telling them how strong they are. These actions affect people the most. It makes them feel loved and, beyond all, appreciated. It also shows that you care about making them feel happy. This note or card will bring a bright smile to their lovely faces.

2. Take Their Favourite Food

"The way to a person's heart is through the stomach," a saying that is quite famous in some parts of the world. Who doesn't feel happy when they get to eat their favorite food. So whoever this person is that you want to make feel loved, on your way back from work, stop by at their favorite restaurant, buy their favorite dish and surprise them with it. Firstly, they will feel loved knowing that you remembered their favorite word and secondly, the food, of course. Now you know whenever someone's feeling low, bring them their favorite food, it'll take their minds off the stressful thing, and they would feel thankful for you.

3. Remind Them Of Their Importance

As easy as it sounds, expressing love is a tricky thing to do. There have been times when we all love someone but don't express it because we feel shy and as a result, they don't feel loved. As everyone grows up, it is easy to feel alone in this world, so always remind people around you how important they are. Tell people you love them, I love you is just a three-word sentence, but the meaning it holds is more profound than the ocean, so don't hesitate and make your loved ones feel loved.

4. Surprise Them

Everyone has different hobbies, and some people like makeup. Someone prefers football over everything else. As everyone is interested in other things, we often hear them talk about these things. Sometimes they talk about how they want something, but they are either saving up for it or don't have the time. Surprise them with things they have talked about and feel excited about. This makes that person feel loved and cared about. They know that you listen to them, and this quality is something that not everyone has.

5. Listen To Them

As I said before, listening is a quality that people often look at in others. We all need that one person who will listen to us and won't interrupt us when we tell them about our day. People feel grateful when they remember that there is still someone that will listen to them no matter what.

6. Include Them In Things That Matter To You

We talked about their interests but remembered you are important too, don't forget about yourself in the process and don't we all know the person who cares about us will always want to know about our lives and support your decisions. So please include them in things that are important to you, fill them in on the ongoing drama of your life, and inform them about your decisions before you take a step ahead.

Conclusion:

When you make someone feel loved, you feel happy, and so do they. Isn't it amazing how easily, by following these steps, you can make someone feel loved? So don't hesitate. Go ahead and show them your love because life's too short to stay hesitant.

Chapter 11:
7 Signs Of An Incompatible Relationship

You might have heard the word 'compatibility' a million times before starting a new relationship or even after getting into one. But what exactly does the word 'compatibility' means? Compatibility is when you and your partner not only share the same interests but also share the same values, goals, have compatible libidos, support each other in their times of distress and frustration, help them achieve their dreams, make each other feel safe, and plan a future where you can both see each other being together and happy. However, not every couple is blessed with the joys of having a compatible relationship. Melody Kiersz, a professional matchmaker, says, "There are some obvious ones, like not wanting the same things in life, lifestyle choices in terms of travel or location, and relationship style (I.e., monogamous vs. Polyamorous)."

No matter how much in love you are with your partner and how desperately you compromise in your relationship to make everything seem better, if you both aren't compatible, then the relationship might have a dead-end in the long run. Here are some signs that will help you see if you are in an incompatible relationship.

1. Your partner doesn't respect the differences:

There's rarely a time when you might feel that you have found a person just like you. People are different from each other. Sometimes, their passion or goals may align with yours, but some differences are always there. You may like to read a book or watch a movie in your free time instead of your partner playing a video game or going outdoor with their friends. If your partner doesn't respect the differences and forces you to change your hobbies and dreams, then it's a red flag. After all, respect is the critical element to any lasting relationship. In an incompatible relationship, your partner might make you feel bad about being different from them and may mock you about the different things you do.

2. Your partner gets overly jealous:

We, as human beings, cannot wholly eliminate the factor of jealousy from within ourselves. Being jealous and possessive of your partner isn't a bad thing, as long as you have it under control. But if your partner gets overly jealous of petty things, keeps a regular check on you and your whereabouts, and constantly bugs you, then it will not only make you frustrated, but you will eventually be exhausted, and your mental health will shamble. This isn't just a sign of incompatibility but also a sign of toxicity.

3. You're a different version of yourself around them:

What is a relationship if you don't even feel comfortable around your partner? Out of all the people, your love interest should be the one with whom you can be yourself and not pretend. You find yourself always pretending to be a perfect flawless creature because they might have said something or showed you that they wouldn't accept the things that your real version does. The constant struggle of making yourself look ideal in

Infront of your partner's eyes would eventually drain you out. You might stop pretending after a while, and your partner may or may not like it. If your partner doesn't like the real you, then you should consider this as an incompatible relationship and move on.

4. Lack of communication:

A lasting relationship is based on communicating effectively with your partner. For example, suppose you feel like your partner discards your feelings and consider them stupid after you tell them that something's been bothering you or tells them that something they've said might have hurt you. In that case, your partner is being emotionally unavailable and doesn't value your feelings. As a result, you might feel uneasy about opening up to them, and they might feel the same about you. This is one of the significant reasons for the incompatibility between the partners. If you aren't ready to share your feelings with them or get ignored if you share them, the relationship will eventually come down the hill.

5. Your partner does not take care of your wants and needs:

Consider this, and you have just come home after a long day of work, hoping to get some rest. As soon as you arrive, there is a long pile of dishes waiting for you, and your partner tells you to make something for dinner. Yep, you can imagine the reaction your partner would get. A relationship should be based on mutual efforts and understanding. If your partner is doing the bare minimum and you find yourself putting in all the efforts, then you definitely don't deserve to be with a person like them. Instead, your partner should treat you special every now and then, makes you realize your worth in his life, takes care of you, and make small gestures to show his love.

6. Fighting gets ugly with them:

Arguing and fighting are the forte of every relationship. What matters is how you resolve the issue after you've argued or fought. In a compatible relationship, couples always try to sort out the things bothering them, and they eventually apologize to each other. While in an incompatible relationship, you would find your partner constantly bickering and mocking long after the fight has ended. You both won't see eye to eye with each other for days and may go to bed angry at each other. Your partner isn't open to change and doesn't respect your views and opinions. You can't agree to disagree with each other and tries to prove the other wrong no matter what. If you find yourself spending more time fighting with your partner than being happy, you clearly are mismatched.

7. Different outlooks on the future:

Two people may be in the same relationship, but they rarely are on the same page. While one might be thinking about getting engaged or married soon, the other might flee to the hills just at the mere name of commitment. One might talk about having kids one day while the other just brushes off the idea that they're not ready for that yet. One must be thinking about traveling the world while the other just wants to stay peacefully in the town. It's best to start talking about your future early in the relationship to see where both of you stand in each other's lives.

Conclusion:

The signs mentioned above are all the major red flags of incompatibility. But, in addition, you must have a sense of mutual respect, understanding, and effort with your partner. For example, suppose you feel that the relationship is one-sided, with you giving your all, making sacrifices, trying to be consistent with them. Yet, at the same time, they couldn't care less about you and don't appreciate or value all that you do for them. In that case, you should consider moving out of the relationship for good.

Chapter 12:

6 Ways On How To Make Your Partner Feel Loved

The word partner has a deep meaning. It means the association with each other. They understand each other, respecting and supporting every step and decision of each other. In simple words, a partner indicates being fully committed to each other.

Being committed includes many challenges, but one of the biggest and the main challenges is how to make your partner feel loved. This is a big challenge because many partners still don't understand each other entirely after spending most of the time together. Efforts from both partners can help in this situation which can lead to a happy and healthy relationship.

Comforting each other in every situation, mostly in their challenging times, has always played a key role in making your partner feel loved. Your partner knows that you are always there to support them and expressing your willingness to make them relieved, and never doubt their decision.

1. Complementing Each Other

Many people think that the female partner in a relationship needs compliments, but the truth is every human being on this planet needs compliments sometimes. Compliments matter a lot, even for boys, but they don't show that they need compliments. Even if they are complimented, they don't show the happiness of being praised. Being praised by a stranger or not so close doesn't matter a lot, but if the compliment comes from an immediate or loved one, it means the world to them. Complimenting each other back and forth can also improve communication, which is the building block.

2. Be Attentive Towards Each Other

Taking each other for granted destroys a relationship. Instead, try to give all of your attention to your partner. It strengthens a connection. It makes them feel wanted. Listen to them with your complete attention. Listen to the first and then give your opinion or comfort them depending on the situation. Pay him the attention the partner deserves because every moment you spend with him is crucial. Whether planning a dinner or a movie night, always carve out time to be with each other. And when you're spending that quality time together, let things flow naturally and give your partner your undivided attention. Show your interest in them and make them feel that you want to be in their company.

3. Little Gestures of Love

Little gestures can also show your partner how much you care about them and make them feel special and loved. Small gestures can include checking on them, texting them, calling them to say how much you miss them, making plans to meet them, sending small meaningful gifts, asking how their day was and what they are doing tomorrow. Plan surprises for them. Randomly say how much you love them. These small gestures will make their day a hundred percent better.

4. Accept That

Acknowledge your partner. Appreciate them for what they are doing for you. Thank them for their attention and their support, and the love they have given. Thank them just for being there.No one is perfect. Everyone has flaws, and those flaws need to be accepted. A person can never be in front of the person they love until and unless the person they love accepts for who they are and accepts their flaws.

5. Appreciate Them

Make them feel special. Make them feel proud of who you have chosen as a partner. Tell them that it was the right decision to choose them as a partner. Send them appreciation paragraphs. Tell them that they are important and they matter and that you cannot take a step or decision without their opinion. Relive and remember your memories with them. Take a trip down memory lane once in a while. Cherish your happy memories, remember you are bad ones too, and promise each other that no more memories like these will ever be made again. Try not to break promises. Try to fulfill them.

6. Excite Each Other Up

Compliment his accomplishments. Tell him that you are proud of what he accomplished and how hard he worked for those accomplishments. Tell him how he deserved what he accomplished.

Conclusion:

Be abundant with happiness. Let your partner lead. Respect him. Be loyal and faithful and give your hundred percent. Be kind and forgive them. Never let your ego win, and never let pride enter your heart.

Chapter 13:

How To Deal With Feeling Anxious In A Relationship

There are different ways in which relationship anxiety can show up. A lot of people, when they are forming a commitment or when they are in the early stages of their relationship, feel a little insecure now; this is not something we would consider unusual, so if you have doubts or fears, you don't need to worry if they are not affecting you a lot. But sometimes, what happens is that these doubts and anxious thoughts creep into your day-to-day life. We will list some of the signs of relationship anxiety so you can figure them out for yourself, and then we will tell you how to deal with them.

1. Wondering if you matter to your partner
2. Worrying they want to breakup
3. Doubting your partners feeling for you
4. Sabotaging the relationship

These are some of the signs of relationship anxiety; now, it can take time to get to the roots of what is causing this. Right now, we will tell you how you can overcome it; yes, you read that right, you can overcome it no matter how hard it feels like at the moment. However, it will take time and consistent effort. The first thing you should do is manage anxiety early as soon as you see the symptoms because you keep delaying it. It will become a problem for you. What will help you is maintaining your identity. When you and your partner start getting closer, you will shift the key parts of your identity to make room for your partner and the relationship. You need to know that this does not help either of you. You will lose yourself, and your partner will lose the person they fell in love with. Secondly, practice good communication. If there is something specific they are doing that is fueling your anxiety, whether it's not making their bed after they wakeup or spending a lot of time on their phone, talk to them about it and try to be non-accusatory and respective about also use I statement these can be a huge help during such conversations. If you feel like things are getting out of control and you will not handle them on your own, talk to a therapist that will get you some clarity. Because it's a relationship issue, try talking to a therapist that works with couples because that can be particularly helpful for you, so if you both have any underlying needs, the therapist will be able to communicate that in a better way.

Chapter 14:

8 Signs You Have Found Your Soulmate

"People think a soulmate is your perfect fit, and that's what everyone wants. But a true soulmate is a mirror, the person who shows you everything that is holding you back, the person who brings you to your attention so you can change your life." - Elizabeth Gilbert.

Legends say that even before you were born, the name of your spiritual half was determined. The two souls roam around the world to find their significant other. Whenever they find one another, they will unite, and their spirits would become one. But finding our long-lost soulmate isn't as easy as we think it is. Out of 7 billion people, it could take some time to find out our perfect match. However, when we meet them, we'll click with them instantly and just know in our hearts that they are made for us. A soulmate is someone you keep coming back to, no matter the struggles, challenges, obstacles, downfalls, or any of the circumstances. Everything would feel perfect with them. But how do you know if someone is your soulmate? You needn't worry! We have compiled for you below the signs that you may have found your soulmate.

1. They would bring the best in you:

Have your friends called you boring or a party pooper since you have entered adult life? Of course, you blame it all on the fact that you have grown up now and have responsibilities. But there's this one person who tends to bring out the fun and sassy side of yours. You feel so comfortable around them that you're even willing to try new things with them. They make your anxiety and fear go away in the blink of an eye. Be it singing songs loudly in the crowd, trying bungee jumping, or just packing up your bags and moving across the country with them to pursue your goals and dreams, they will strengthen you by supporting your decisions and being there for you.

2. They won't play games with you:

They won't be inconsistent with you, like making you feel special one day and ignoring you completely the next. You won't be questioning his feelings about you or putting yourself in a state of over-thinking. Sure, they won't make grand gestures like showing up at your window holding a guitar at 3 in the morning or putting up a billboard saying how much they love you (although we will happily accept both). Still, they will make you realize your worth in their life by always prioritizing you, making you happy, asking about you throughout the day, and paying close attention to whatever you say.

3. You respect each other's differences:

When starting a new relationship, people tend to avoid or hold back specific thoughts, beliefs, or opinions. This is because, in the game of love, both of the couple's emotions are at stake. They don't speak their mind until and unless they're entirely comfortable with their partner. Your soulmate would always be open to change and respect your opinions and views, even if they disagree. They wouldn't ever implement their beliefs and ideas on you but would instead find comfort in knowing that you both don't have the same set of minds. It's essential to be on the same page with your partner on certain things, like the future, life goals, children, etc., but it's okay to have different moral and political views, as long as you both respect each other and it doesn't hurt the other's sentiments.

4. You forgive each other:

Being soulmates doesn't save you from the wrath of arguments and fights. Every relationship experiences indifference and frustration from time to time. But it is one of the things that makes your bond stronger with your partner. You both would rather sit and try to talk it through or sort it out instead of going to bed angry at each other. And when it comes to forgiving the other, you both would do it in a heartbeat. You wouldn't consider holding the other person guilty and would make unique gestures to try and make it up with them.

5. You give each other space:

Your partner doesn't constantly bug you by texting and calling you every minute. They don't ask you about your whereabouts and don't act overly possessive. And rightly so, you do the same with them. You give each other your space and know that the other person would always be there for you. Even if you have to ask them about some distance, they respect it without complaining. You both trust each other with your whole heart and respect them enough to give them the space they have asked for.

6. You empathize with each other:

If your soulmate tells you about them getting good grades in college, finding their dream job, or getting a promotion, you find yourself being more excited and happier for them than they are. Sometimes, we feel drained out by showing too much empathy to other people and understanding and friendly. But with your soulmate, you don't have to force it out or pretend, and it just comes naturally. Whenever they feel scared or anxious, you're right there with them, protecting them from the world and not leaving their side until you make sure they're okay.

7. You communicate with each other effectively:

They say that communication is essential for any long-lasting relationship. If you aren't communicating well with your partner, you might find yourself in the depths of overthinking the worst-case scenarios. Your partner makes it easy for you to share with them, even if you hadn't done the deed before. You find yourself talking about the tough things, the things that bother you or hurt you, and they comfort and console you reassure you that they will fix it. Similarly, you make sure your partner speaks your mind to you, and you do your best to right your wrongs and clear any of their doubts.

8. You have seen each other's flaws and still loves each other the same:

It isn't easy to accept someone with the habits or traits that you despise. However, you have been your complete and utter authentic version of yourself with them, and they still love you the same. Be it crying loudly while watching an emotional sitcom, binge eating at night, snoring, burping, or just showing them your weak and vulnerable phase when you tend to push everyone away and dress up like a homeless drug addict. They find your quirks cute and accept you with all your imperfections and flaws, and you do the same with them.

Conclusion:

A soulmate is someone who makes you realize your worth and brings out the best in you. They might drive you crazy, ignites your triggers, stirs your passions, but they might also be your most excellent teacher. They would allow you to discover your true self while always being there for you and supporting you all the way.

Chapter 15:

<u>Ten Signs You're Falling In Love</u>

As our Literature master, Shakespeare, once said, 'A heart to love, and in that heart, courage, to make's love known.'

Ah, love! A four-lettered small word that leaves such a heavy impact on people. Falling in love is nothing short of a beautiful experience, but it can also give you a veritable roller-coaster of emotions. From feeling unsure to terrifying, disgusting, exhilarating, and excited, you might feel it all. If your mobile screen pops up and you're hoping to see their name on the screen, or you're looking for their face in a crowd full of thousands, then you, my child, are doomed! You are well familiar with the feeling of getting butterflies just by hearing their voice, the urge to change your wardrobe completely to impress them, the constant need to be with them all the time. It is known that people who are in love tend to care about the other person's needs as they do their own.

You often go out of their way for their happiness. Whether it's something as small as making their favorite dish or impressing them with some grand gestures, you always try to make them feel content and happy.

If you're in the middle of some casual inquiry into whether you're falling in love, then we are here to help you. Below are some signs for you to discover if it's really just simply a loss of appetite or if you're merely lovesick.

1. You don't hesitate to try new things with them:

One of the factors that you could look into is that you become fearless and more adventurous when you are in love. You don't hang back to step out of your comfort zone and engage in all your partner favors' activities and interests. Suddenly the idea of trying sushi or wearing something bright doesn't seem so crazy. You are willing to be more daring and open to new experiences. You are ready to go on that spontaneous trip with them and make memories, all while being a little scared inside. But isn't love all about trying new things with your partner? The New York Times article in 2008 revealed that people in a relationship who try new hobbies together help keep the spark alive long after the honeymoon phase is over.

2. You're always thinking about them:

When you are in love, you always tend to think about your partner. Rehash your last conversation with them, or simply smiling at something they said, or questions like what they must be doing right now, have they eaten their meal yet, did they go to work on time or were late again, are always on the back of your mind. You are mentally, emotionally, and physically impacted about caring for them. But it isn't overwhelming. Instead, you get a sense of a calm and secure reality that you will constantly crave. When in love, we tend to merge with that person in such a way that they start to dominate our thoughts and we become wholly preoccupied with them.

3. You become anxious and stressed:

According to a psychology study, falling in love could also cause higher levels of cortisol, a stress home, in your body. So the next time you feel jittery or anxious, that person might mean more to you than you think. You might become anxious to dress up nicely to impress them, or if they ask you something, the pressure of answering them intellectually can be expected. But suppose you're feeling overly anxious about your partner, like them not texting you back instantly or thinking they might be cheating on you. In that case, it's an indication of insecure attachment, and you might want to work on yourself to avoid feeling like this.

4. You become inspired and motivated:

A few days ago, you needed the motivation to get out of bed. And now, the future suddenly seems so bright and full of potential. Your partner inspires you to set up new goals, have a positive attitude, and cheer you from behind while you feel full of energy and chase them. When we are in love, a part of our brain, considered the reward system, releases excess dopamine, and we feel invincible, omnipotent, and daring. Your life becomes significantly better when you're around them.

5. You become empathetic towards them:

It's not a secret that you start seeing your partner as an extension of yourself and reciprocate whatever they feel when you fall in love. Suppose they are accepted into their favorite program, or they expect to receive that interview call, or their favorite football team might have lost in the quarters. In that case, you might feel the same excitement, happiness, or distress that your partner does. Becoming empathetic towards your partner means making sacrifices for them, like going to the grocery store because your partner is tired or refueling their tank in the cold so that they don't have to step out. According to an expert, "Your love is growing when you have an increased sense of empathy toward your partner. When they feel sad, you feel sad. When they feel happy, you feel happy. This might mean going out of the way to give them love in the way that they want to receive it, even if it is not the way you would want to receive love."

6. It's just plain easy:

You don't have to put in extra effort, and it doesn't seem to drain your energy. Instead, you feel energized and easy. You can be your complete, authentic self around them. And it always just seems to go with the flow. Even the arguments don't feel much heated as they did in the other relationships. When you're in love, you prioritize your partner over your pride and ego. You don't hesitate to apologize to them and keep your relationship above everything. When you are with your partner, and it doesn't feel like hard work, know that they are the one!

7. You crave their presence:

Some theorists say that we are more drawn to kissing, hugging, and physical touch when we fall in love. Physical closeness releases a burst of the love hormone termed Oxytocin, which helps us feel bonded. Of course, you don't want to come as someone too clingy who is permanently attached to his partner's hip, but knowing where your person is or how their day went is what you should be looking forward to. On the flipside, Corticotrophin is released as part of a stress response when we are away from our partner, which can contribute to anxiety and depression.

8. You feel safe around them:

It takes a lot of courage for people to open up to their partners. If you don't mind being vulnerable around them, or if you've opened up to them about your dark past or addressed your insecurities, and they have listened contently to you and reassured you. You have done vice versa with your partner, then that's just one of the many signs that you both are in love with each other. Long-lasting love gives you a solid ground and a safe space where you can be upset and vulnerable. When we feel an attachment to our partner, our brain releases the hormones vasopressin and Oxytocin, making us feel secure.

9. You want to introduce them to your family and friends:

You just never shut up about your love interest over the family dinner or when hanging out with your friends. They know all about them, from their favorite spot in the city to the color of their eyes, to how much you adore them and want to spend every single minute talking about them. And now all your family members and friends are curious to meet the guy/girl they have been listening about for the past few weeks. You want to introduce them into every aspect of your life and want it to last this time. So, you make perfect arrangements for them to meet your friends and family, and on the other hand, threatens them to behave Infront of him/her.

10. You care about their happiness:

When you put them and their feelings first, that's how you know it's true love. You don't just want happiness for yourself only, but instead wants it in excess measure for your partner. According to marriage researchers at UC Berkeley, " Spouses who love each other stay together longer, be happier, and support each other more effectively than couples who do not love each other compassionately." You want to go out of your way, or do their favorite thing, to see a smile on their face.

Conclusion:

If you relate to the signs above, then you've already been hit by the love cupid. Scientists have discovered that falling in love, is in fact, a real thing. The brain releases Phenylethylamine, a hormone known for creating feelings of infatuation towards your significant other. The mix and match of different hormones released in our body while we are in love are wondrous. If you have gotten lucky and found a special someone for yourself, then cling to them and don't let them go! If you found this video helpful, please like and subscribe to the channel. Also don't forget to share this video with someone who you find might benefit from this topic as well!

Chapter 16:

How To Focus on Creating Positive Actions

Only a positive person can lead a healthy life. Imagine waking up every day feeling like you are ready to face the day's challenges and you are filled with hope about life. That is something an optimist doesn't have to imagine because they already feel it every day. Also, scientifically, it is proven that optimistic people have a lower chance of dying because of a stress-caused disease. Although positive thinking will not magically vanish all your problems, it will make them seem more manageable and somewhat not a big deal.

Positive thinking is what leads to positive actions, actions that affect you and the people around you. When you think positively, your actions show how positive you are. You can create positive thinking by focusing on the good in life, even if it may feel tiny thing to feel happy about because when you once learn to be satisfied with minor things, you would think that you no longer feel the same amount of stress as before and now you would feel freer. This positive attitude will always find the good in everything, and life would seem much easier than before.

Being grateful for the things you have contributed a lot to your positive behavior. Gratitude has proven to reduce stress and improve self-esteem. Think of the things you are grateful for; for example, if someone gives you good advice, then be thankful to them, for if someone has helped you with something, then be grateful to them, by being grateful about minor things, you feel more optimistic about life, you feel that good things have always been coming to you. Studies show that making down a list of things you are grateful for during hard days helps you survive through the tough times.

A person laughing always looks like a happy person. Studies have shown that laughter lowers stress, anxiety, and depression. Open yourself up to humor, permit yourself to laugh even if forced because even a forced laugh can improve your mood. Laughter lightens the mood and makes problems seem more manageable. Your laughter is contagious, and it may even enhance the perspective of the people around us.

People with depression or anxiety are always their jailers; being harsh on themselves will only cause pain, negativity, and insecurity. So try to be soft with yourself, give yourself a positive talk regularly; it has proven to affect a person's actions. A positive word to yourself can influence your ability to regulate your feelings and thoughts. The positivity you carry in your brain is expressed through your actions, and who doesn't loves an optimistic person. Instead of blaming yourself, you can think differently, like "I will do better next time" or "I can fix this." Being optimistic about the complicated situation can lead your brain to find a solution to that problem.

When you wake up, it is good to do something positive in the morning, which mentally freshens you up. You can start the day by reading a positive quote about life and understand the meaning of that quote, and you may feel an overwhelming feeling after letting the meaning set. Everybody loves a good song, so start by listening to a piece of music that gives you positive vibes, that gives you hope, and motivation for the day. You can also share your positivity by being nice to someone or doing something nice for someone; you will find that you feel thrilled and positive by making someone else happy.

Surely you can't just start thinking positively in a night, but you can learn to approach things and people with a positive outlook with some practice.

Chapter 17:

8 Ways To Make The Sex Good

Has your sex life gone stale? Between kids, work, financial pressures, and all the other stressful things, steamy sex may seem like nothing but a fantasy.

Sex isn't just fun, but it's healthy for you too. Every orgasm releases a burst of oxytocin, which instantly improves your mood. Regular rolls in the hay could also improve your heart health, improve your self-esteem, reduce stress and depression, and help you sleep better. As little as only snuggling together underneath the sheets also make you feel closer to your partner and can enhance your sense of intimacy.

If you're stuck in a sexual rut, trust me, you're not alone. While dry spells are expected in any relationship, it's still no consolation for couples experiencing one. The more we get used to someone, the less exciting sex becomes, as familiarity is the death of sex drive. Treating sexual problems is easier now than ever before.

Here are some quick tips to help you reignite the passion your sex life is lacking.

1. Stop Feeling Insecure About Your Body

It really doesn't matter if you haven't lost the baby weight, your specific body parts aren't as high as they used to be, or you have a pimple the size of an egg; it doesn't matter at all. When you're in bed and making love, your partners are not worried about any of your imperfections. To him, you're still the sexiest lady he fell in love with. Besides, it would be best if you understood that his body isn't perfect either. He might have a large belly or a body full of hair. But he doesn't let it get in the way of a good time, and you shouldn't either.

2. Mark A Date

Scheduling sex might sound controlling and not at all fun, but sometimes planning is in order. You book time in your calendar for many things, so why not do the same to prioritize sex? You have to make some room for it and push it forward. Reconnecting with your partner will remind you why you got attracted to him in the first place. Once you have made that sex appointment, the anticipation can be almost as titillating as the event. So, trade some racy texts or leave a sultry voicemail on his cell.

3. Use Lubrication

Often, the vaginal dryness can lead to painful sex, which can, in turn, lead to flagging libido and growing relationship tensions. To avoid any pain during sex or hurting yourself resulting from it, use lubricating liquids and gels. This will make the sex painless and turn on both of you more and more.

4. Practice Touching

Sex therapists use sensate focus techniques that can help you re-establish physical intimacy without feeling pressured. Many of the self-help books and educational videos offer many variations on such exercises. You can also ask your partner to touch you in a manner that you would like to be touched by them, or ask them how they want to be touched. This will give you an idea of the range of pressure from gentle to firm that you should use.

5. Try Different Positions

Sometimes, couples get bored by trying the same 2-3 positions over and over again. Searching and trying new positions will definitely spice up your love life. Developing a repertoire of different sexual positions can enhance your experience of lovemaking and add interest and help you overcome problems. For example, when a man enters his partner from behind, the increased stimulation to the G-spot can help a woman reach orgasm faster.

6. Write Down Your Fantasies

This exercise can help you explore endless possibilities that you think might turn on you and your partner. It could be anything, from reading an erotic book to watching an aroused scene from a movie or TV show that turned you on, you could re-enact them with your partner. Similarly, you could ask your partner about their fantasies and help them fulfill them. This activity is also helpful for people with low desires.

7. Do Kegel Exercises

Both men and women should improve their sexual fitness by exercising their pelvic floor muscles. To do these exercises, tighten the muscle you would use while trying to stop urine in midstream. Hold the contraction for two or three seconds, then release. Repeat 10 times of five sets a day. These exercises can be done anywhere while driving, sitting at your desk, or standing in a check-out line. At home, women may use vaginal weights to add muscle resistance.

8. Try To Relax

Do something soothing and relaxing together before having sex instead of jumping right into it (not that you can't do that), such as playing a game, watching a movie, or having a nice candlelight dinner.

Conclusion

Lack of communication is often what leads to sex droughts in a relationship. Even if you are sexually mismatched, you can get creative and fix those inequities. Stress and busyness of life, among other factors, can also affect sexual intimacy, but there are fruitful ways to overcome setbacks. Don't let fear or embarrassment stop you from trying new stuff. Tap into something simple to get back on track.

Chapter 18:

7 Ways To Forgive You Partner

Forgiveness usually means to stop being angry or to stop blaming someone who made a mistake. Forgive and let go of it hurts a lot in a relationship, but it is also essential to keep it happy and healthy.

1. Take Your time To Forgive

Ask your partner to give you some space. You were able to forgive needs some time. It involves patience and trust. Sit alone and think about it. Think about how and why you are going to forgive your partner. Make up your mind for everything. Make your mind up for any further challenges or consequences. Think about how you are going to tell him what's in your mind and heart. If you can't think alone, ask a friend for advice. Get consultation if needed.

2. Forgiveness Helps You Heal

Holding onto resentment can sour you and keep you from finding peace. When you can't forgive, your emotional wounds can't close and heal. Forgiveness allows you to let go of pain and continue with a lighter heart. Forgiveness, in other words, enables you to begin moving away from anger and resentment before they seep into all areas of your life.

3. Talk When You Are Ready

Honest communication is vital at this juncture. Sit together. Tell your partner what's been on your mind. Let them know how you feel and how much it has affected you. Tell them that the word forgive means that the person who did something will never do this again. If they agree that what they did will never do it again will then be ignored. Also, ask your partner what they are feeling and how they are coping with this situation. Ask them how they want this relationship to be healthy. You can't truly forgive without empathy and compassion. Committing to forgiveness is only the beginning, and memories of your hurt may still resurface after you've decided to ignore it. Holding on to understanding and patience can help you succeed.

4. Forgive But Don't Forget

Forgiving your partner for what they did is a crucial step, and forgiving can achieve it, but forgetting is the hard part. It is not like you should forget what happened, but forgetting can be attained by redefining boundaries in a way that will let your relationship move past a setback and start a new chapter. Rebuilding trust essentially happens through actions, not words.

5. Forgiveness Helps You Reconcile

You can forgive someone even if you know you can never have the same relationship. Depending on the circumstances, you may even need to avoid contact. That said, everyone makes mistakes. When a loved one hurts you, forgiving them can open the door to relationship repair. In many cases, the act of forgiveness can help someone who inadvertently caused pain to realize how they hurt you. This provides an opportunity for learning and growth. Forgiveness may not mend your relationship immediately, but it's a good start.

6. Find The Bright Side

When someone hurts you, you're probably not in a position to notice any benefits that came out of the situation. In time, you may have more emotional space to recognize what you've gained. Even when you can't identify a clear benefit, you may feel like a better person for embracing compassion and understanding.

7. Try To Move On

You can't ignore the challenges life throws at you. But prioritizing compassion and empathy can make it easier to notice the good things and give them more weight than the bad. If something positive did come out of it, you already have some practice finding the flower amongst the rubble. You don't have to believe that everything has meaning or happens because of destiny. You can make your meaning and find your good, no matter what life brings.

Conclusion:

It's normal to want someone to regret the pain they inflicted. The truth is, this doesn't always happen. Some people aren't capable of recognizing when they cause pain. Others don't see their mistakes or don't care. You may never get an explanation or an apology. Letting bitterness and resentment maintain a hold over you only gives them power. Instead of letting the past hold you back, use what you learned from the experience to take steps to protect yourself from future pain.

Chapter 19:

6 Ways To Deal With Gaslighting In A Relationship

We call it gas lighting when someone manipulates you into thinking that you are confused about your feelings or when someone makes you doubt them. It is crucial to know if you are gaslit in a relationship to break that chain of toxicity. It leaves you with doubts as well as insecurities within yourself. So good to end it as soon as possible. People gaslight others to make sure that you do what they want. You will notice that gradually you do things that they would like you to do. They manipulate you into doing what they like.

People who gaslight others in a relationship trivialize their feelings. They will address your even tiniest of feelings as overreacting. They try to control the situation their way. Changing details about something that happened in the past and constantly blames you for everything they did. When it comes to your needs or wants, they frequently change the subject, ensuring that you always think about what they would like or want. They keep you low on the priority list while they keep themselves upon yours. All we need is to be safe from these kinds of people. For that, the following are the ways to deal with gaslighting.

1. **Confirm Manipulation**

People may confuse someone's rude behavior or childish behavior with gaslighting. It's not always necessarily true that the other person is gaslighting. It might be their true nature to talk with an attitude. It is commonly mistaken for gaslighting in a relationship. Gaslighting is the repetitive behavior of deceiving or manipulation the same person. If the person is not polite towards you, then it may not be considered manipulation in any way. People may gaslight you unintentionally too. When they say something in the heat of the moment, it doesn't necessarily mean they want to manipulate you.

2. Speak Up

When you stay quiet in times of raising your voice, then it becomes a habit. When they know that you won't speak up to them about their behavior, they burden you more. You get habitual of not speaking back, and they get habitual of getting away with manipulation or lies every time. Show them that you won't accept the way they treat you. They will eventually find their mistake or find out that it was not worth it.

3. Stay Self-Assured

When a manipulative person tries to change the small details about any event, you need to be confident in your version of the story you think happened. When they see you constantly hesitating, then they become more confident in their version. They will start making you doubt yourself in a way that whatever they say sounds true. You need to be firm on your point and make them see that you know the truth of the situation.

4. Self-Aid

No matter what you think is vital in your life, it would be best if you were your priority, always. Self-aid or self-care is extremely important for a person to follow with or without a relationship. A gaslighting person will always try to make themselves your priority. In that case, you need to stand your ground and show them that you come first in every aspect of your life. With self-care, you will be active mentally and physically. You will get the power to fight for yourself.

5. Communicate With Friends

It's more reliable to talk to others about your situation. When you are confused about your partner's behavior, you can always ask for support from someone you trust. They will help you get a better idea of the situation you are in and maybe help you get out of it. Third-party who knows both sides of the story will help you sort out your relationship.

6. Administrative Support

It is always helpful to seek professional knowledge from people as they know much better than us and understand the situation much more clearly. Ask them for help. They will professionally help you out and make sure you are okay. Gaslighting is not to be taken lightly. Professional service will always be available for those who feel like reaching out for it. There is no embarrassment in seeking executive help.

Conclusion:

There are lots of people who are suffering from gaslighting. If you think that you are one of them, then you need to follow each step carefully. Make sure that you feel safe and sound in your life. The person gaslighting will eventually make their mistake but don't wait for them too. Get out of that toxic relationship as soon as possible.

Chapter 20:

12 Things to Do When You Feel Overwhelmed

Sometimes we get overwhelmed and are completely clueless as to what we should do the trick with that it is to reset quickly so you can recover and get back to what you need to do and things you have to do. Here are 12 of the best tactics to make that happen.

1. Take An Emotional Time Out

Try reading an engaging book that is not related to the work you are currently doing or go and watch a nice movie. The goal here is to take an hour and two away from your problems- physically someplace else if that is possible. This will help you remember that there is a vast world out there and will put you back in perspective.

2. Take A Physical Time Out

Make yourself move a bit; you can hit the gym or go for a run or swim, take a dance class, whatever it is you do for exercise, try to work it in the middle of the day; that way, you will be able to separate your difficult morning from the rest of your day. Once more, you can emotionally separate   yourself   from   your   worries.

3. Breathe Deeply

This is a shorter and much more effective and practical way. All you need to do is take a full 120 seconds to breathe in and out very deeply, maybe go for 6 or 7 breaths per minute, and by the end, you will feel a bit better than before.

4. Be Mindfully Thankful

If you are here right now reading this, you should be thankful you are alive at one of the greatest times, using a device that lets you connect with the entire history of the world's knowledge basically for free and with just one click. Hopefully, you have people in your life that love you. Even if you do not realize it right away, you still have people like that in your life. You know what? Things are pretty good, no matter how rough they might seem at any particular moment. Take a minute, reflect, and reset.

5. Pray Or Meditate

Whatever is your way of connecting with the higher power, you should spend a few minutes daily doing it. This will be important for you in the process of grounding, and you will stay connected to your surroundings.

6. Phone A Friend

Sometimes all you need is a chance to talk with someone you're close with who is completely unrelated to whatever momentary drama is going on in your life. Catching up with old buddies can be refreshing. It can remind you of all the good time you have spent and gives you a break from whatever is currently going on in your life.

7. Delegate

Do you have to do it all yourself? If the answer is no, then don't. Share the load. And don't forget, you don't have to be the boss to delegate. You can often simply ask colleagues and friends for help. They'll give you the chance to return the favor sometime.

8. Write Stuff Down

Sometimes things become more manageable when you write them down. A top military officer I knew kept a journal during the invasion of Iraq. He was so worried and stressed that he only had time to write one haiku per day, but it helped him keep his head on straight.

9. Take A Nap

Everything looks a bit better in the morning and also after you have taken a 30-min catnap. This might not be the most practical suggestion if you work for someone else, but if you're your own boss, then it's perfect you can do things on your own terms, which means you can sneak a nap in between work.

10. Map Your Progress

Create a to-do list in which you can include things you have already done. All you have to do is go back and cross those things out. You will be able to put in perspective how much you have achieved in a day, especially on a particularly rough day.

11. Drink (Water)

Studies have shown increasing your water intake improves your mood. Even though it's supposed to take longer than just drinking a bottle or two, I find that water has a placebo effect. It makes you feel better because you know you're doing something small that's health-positive.

12. Turn Stuff Down

Sometimes you just need to say no. Sometimes you even have to say, "I know I said yes before--but I have to say no now." Of course, you don't want to do a practice this and develop a reputation for unreliability. Still, maybe it's better than getting overwhelmed and getting nothing done.

Chapter 21:

10 Habits of Happy People

Happy people live the most satisfying lives on the planet. They have come to understand the importance of not worrying because it will not make any differential change in their lives. If you cannot control the outcome of a process, why worry? If you can control and make a difference to the outcome of a situation, why worry? Worrying does not bring an ounce of success your way.

Here are 10 habits of happy people that could be you if you choose to adopt it:

1. Happy People Count Their Blessings.

Taking stock of your successes is an important part of appreciating yourself. You find comfort in knowing that despite all the hiccups you have found in your journey there remains an oasis of achievements in your desert.

Everyone needs to take stock of what is in his or her basket of blessings. It is a reminder of your resilience and persistence in the face of challenges. It is an indication of your ability and a minute representation of the progress you can make, given time.

Remind yourself of the taste of victory in your small achievements. It begins with understanding that you definitely cannot be able to win it all. There are grey and shadow areas that will not be within your reach.

2. Happy People Do Not Need the Validation of Others.

Happy people do not wait for the validation of other people. They are autonomous. Develop the habit of doing what is right regardless of your audience and you will have an authentic lifestyle. As such, your source of happiness will be independent of uncontrollable factors. Why should you tie your happiness to someone else capable of ruining your day in a snap? This is not to mean that you will not need other people. Humans are social beings and interdependent. Letting them strongly influence your lifestyle is the major problem. Be your own man.

3. They Are Bold.

Boldly and cautiously pursuing their ambitions is part of the ingredients that make up happy people. Knowing what you want is one thing and pursuing it is another. If music is your passion and it makes you happy, chase after it for it is therein that your happiness lies. Whatever it is (of course considering its legality) do not let it pass.

To be truly happy, do not live in the shadow of other happy people. Define your happiness and drink from your well. Timidity will make you bask under the shade of giants and create a sense of false security. One day the shade will be no more and leave you exposed to an unimaginable reality.

4. <u>They are social people.</u>

Being social is one common characteristic of happy people. Happiness makes them bubbly and alive. There is a common testament in almost all happy people – either happiness made them social or their social nature made them happy. Thanks to whichever of the two came earlier, they are happy people!

Like bad luck, happiness is contagious. Your social circle can infect you with happiness or even deny it to you. Being sociable does not mean to the extreme nature with all the hype that comes along.

It means being approachable to people. Some will positively add to your basket and others will offer positive criticism towards your cause. With such input, your happiness will have longevity.

5. <u>Believe in a greater cause.</u>

Happy people understand that it is not always about them. There is a greater cause above their interests. They do not derive their happiness from the satisfaction of their needs and wants. Regardless of any deficiency in their lives, their flame of happiness is not easily put out.

Do you want to be happy? It is time to put self-interest aside and not tie your happiness to local anchors. An average person's happiness is mainly dependent on his well-being. Refusing to be average gives you leverage over those out to put off your happiness.

6. <u>Lead a purposeful life.</u>

Are there happy people without purpose? Those we see happy maintain their status by having a powerful drive towards the same. A strong purpose will make you stay on happiness' lane. It is the habit of happy people to have a purpose. This is to enable them to stay on course.

Being happy is not a permanent state. It is easily reversible if caution is not taken. Purposefulness is part of the caution taken by happy people.

7. Admit they are human.

To err is human. Given this, happy people appreciate the erroneous nature of man and accept the things they cannot change, have the courage to change the things they can, and the wisdom to know the difference. A prayer commonly referred to as the serenity prayer.

Admitting being human is the first step towards being happy. You forgive yourself of your wrongs before seeking the forgiveness of another. This brings inner peace culminating in happiness.

8. Know their strengths and weaknesses.

Being aware of your strengths and weaknesses is one thing happy people have mastered. Through that, they know their limits; the time to push and time to take a break. This serves to help avoid unwarranted disappointments that come along with new challenges.

Nothing can put off the charisma of a prepared spirit. Happy people know their limitations well enough such that no ill-willed voice can whisper disappointments to them. They hold the power of self-awareness within their hearts making them live with contentment.

9. Notice the contributions of those around them.

No man is an island. The contributions of other people in our lives cannot be emphasized enough. We are because they are (for all the good reasons). At any one point in our lives, someone made us happy. The first step is noticing the roles played by those in our immediate environment.

The joy of being surrounded by people to hold our hands in life is engraved deeper in our hearts in times of need. It is time you stop looking far away and turn your eyes to see what is next to you.

10. They are grateful and appreciative.

"Thank you" is a word that does not depart from the lips of happy people. Their hearts are trained to focus on what is at their disposal instead of what they cannot reach. It is crystal that a bird in hand is worth two in the bush.

Happy people continue being happy despite deficiencies. Try being appreciative and see how happiness will tow along.

Adopt these 10 habits of happy people and depression will keep away from you. If you want to be happy, do what happy people do and you will see the difference.

Chapter 22:

8 Signs You Need to Call it Quits

Intro:

Most of the times, we stretch our relationship to the point that it becomes unbearable for us to be with someone. We either fear uncertainty or be lonely that we push our boundaries of tolerance; the sole reason for doing that is to avoid pain. You need to take care of your happiness. The whole point of being with someone is to be happy. If there is no passion or romance left and your relationship feels stagnant, it is time for you to call it quits because from that point on, your relationship is only going to degrade, and you should leave before things take a turn for the worse. If you feel that you deserve better and have unmet emotional needs, there is no reason to continue the relationship. Even if you try your hardest, you can not twist the reality. If you are having trouble figuring out whether you should call it quits or not, we are going to give you 7 reasons why you should call it quits!

1. Lost Trust:

One of the essential parts of a relationship is "trust" it works like glue and holds a relationship together. Trust assures you that a person is loyal to you, and no matter what happens, they will always stay by your side. The long-term survival of a relationship is not possible without trust. If you do not trust your partner, you will doubt their actions, and it will be bad for you and them because you will be acting like a detective checking upon them all the time, they will lose their freedom, and you will lose your peace of mind. If you do not trust your partner, you should just let them go.

2. You feel Unhappy:

All relationships feel amazing in the beginning. Later, you get to see their partner for who they are. The point of getting into a relationship is to feel happy and complete. If you feel anxious and full of pain, then what is the point of this relationship? You will start feeling lonely even when your partner is with you. If you feel sad and disappointed most of the time rather than happy and sad, it just means your partner does not think about you anymore. If you need to leave your partner to find peace, then it's time to call it quits.

3. Lack of Support:

It is essential to have a supportive and understanding partner if you want your relationship to grow. Your relationship becomes ten times harder if your partner does not believe in your dreams most of your time and energy will be consumed in convincing them that you are capable of doing that. If someone important in your life will continuously discourage you, negativity and self-doubt will surround you. Being with the wrong person will make you feel worthless all the time. If someone is hindering your growth and pulling you down, then you should cut them loose.

4. Zero Communication:

Lack of communication will lead to a lot of misunderstandings. If you do not sit with your partner to speak your mind with them, your emotions are bottled up and even when you do, they do not try to understand your perspective and instead play blame games this just results in hurting you more. If there is increased misunderstanding and you have tried to solve the issue multiple times, and the result is always the same, there is a high chance things are not going to change in the near future. There is a difference between not trying to communicate and not trying to understand the other person. If the case is later, then it's time to leave them for good.

5. Controlling Behavior:

It might be a bit difficult for you to identify between a caring partner and a controlling partner. But we are here to make things easy for you. A controlling partner always interferes in your business and will criticize you even for little things. The worst thing they will do is isolate you from your family and friends, and sometimes they will even try to turn them against you. They are insecure, so they will also ask you to not talk to certain people, mostly of the opposite gender. Plus, you will have to explain yourself a lot, and if you do not, it will lead to a fight.

6. Zero Efforts:

The key factor that leads to the growth of a relationship is an active effort from both sides. It is all in the efforts you make to get to know them, keep each other happy and take an interest in each other's life. A relationship does not survive if there is not enough effort from both sides. If there is a one-sided effort, then there will be a lot of burden on the person trying to make it work, and as a result, this will drain your energy and exhaust yourself. If your partner does not go beyond their comfort zone to be there for you will suffocate you.

7. Different Life Paths:

If you and your partner are on the same page, the relationship will go a long way. At first, you do not really care about the future because you are so engrossed in your relationship, but when you realize that this might affect your goals, it is difficult to carry on. You will think about it every day, and it will consume you, but you should remember no relationship is greater than your happiness.

Conclusion:

All of the relationships and people are different from each other some choose to leave a relationship for their dreams, and some might give up their dreams for love. What you need to do is find out what makes you happy and works for you. You need to set limits for yourself, and beyond those limits, you will not compromise or bend yourself. You should never forget the entire point of being in a relationship is to be happy, and so you can finally have someone who understands you. These are the two things you should never compromise on.

Chapter 23:
Happy People Are Busy but Not Rushed

Dan Pink points to an interesting new research finding — the happiest people are those that are very busy but don't feel rushed:

Who among us are the happiest? Newly published research suggests that fortunate folks have little or no excess time and yet seldom feel rushed.

This clicks with me. I love blogging, but I hate being under time pressure to get it done. This tension is very nicely demonstrated in a recent study by Hsee et al. (2010). When given a choice, participants preferred to do nothing unless given the tiniest possible reason to do something: a piece of candy. Then they sprang into action.

Not only did people only need the smallest inducement to keep busy, but they were also happier when doing something rather than nothing. It's as if people understand that being busy will keep them happier, but they need an excuse of some kind.

Having plenty of time gives you a feeling of control. Anything that increases your *perception of control* over a situation (whether it increases your control or not) can substantially decrease your stress level.

In Colorado, Steve Maier at the University of Boulder says that the degree of control that organisms can exert over something that creates stress determines whether the stressor alters the organism's functioning. His findings indicate that only uncontrollable stressors cause harmful effects. Inescapable or uncontrollable stress can be destructive, whereas the same stress that feels escapable is less destructive, significantly so... Over and over, scientists see that the perception of control over a stressor alters the stressor's impact.

But heavy time pressure stresses you out and kills creativity. Low-to-moderate time pressure produces the best results.

If managers regularly set impossibly short time-frames or impossibly high workloads, employees become stressed, unhappy, and unmotivated—burned out. Yet, people hate being bored. It was rare for any participant in our study to report a day with very low time pressure, such days—when they did occur—were also not conducive to positive inner work life. In general, low-to-moderate time pressure seems optimal for sustaining positive thoughts, feelings, and drives.

Your reaction to being too busy and under time pressure might be to want to do nothing. But that can drop you into the bottom left corner. And this makes you more unhappy than anything:

...surveys "continue to show the least happy group to be those who quite often have excess time." Boredom, it seems, is burdensome.

So, stay busy—set goals. Challenge yourself, but make sure you have plenty of time to feel in control of the situation.

This is how games feel. And games are fun.

Chapter 24:

6 Signs You Are Emotionally Unavailable

In times of need, all we want is emotional comfort. The people around us mainly provide it. But the question is, will we support them if the need arises? You might be emotionally unavailable for them when they need you. It is necessary to have some emotional stability to form some strong bonds. If you are emotionally unapproachable, you will have fewer friends than someone you stand mentally tall. It is not harmful to be emotionally unavailable, but you need to change that in the long run. And for that, you need to reflect on yourself first.

It would help if you always were your top priority. While knowing why you are emotionally unapproachable, you need to focus on yourself calmly. Giving respect and talking is not enough for someone to rely on you. You need to support them whenever needed. Talk your mind with them. Be honest with them. But not in a rude way, in a comforting way. So, next time they will come to you for emotional support and comfort. If you are relating to all these things, then here are some signs that confirm it.

1. You Keep People At A Distance

It is usual for an emotionally unavailable person to be seen alone at times. They tend to stay aloof at times; that way, they don't have to be emotionally available. And even if you meet people, you always find it challenging to make a bond with them. You might have a few friends and family members close to you. But you always find meeting new people an emotionally draining activity. You also might like to hang out with people, but opening up is not your forte. If you are emotionally unavailable, then you keep people at a hands distance from you.

2. You Have Insecurities

If you struggle to love yourself, then count it as a sign of emotional stress. People are likely to be unavailable emotionally for others when they are emotionally unavailable for themselves too. We always doubt the people who love us. How can they when I, myself, can't? And this self-hatred eventually results in a distant relationship with your fellow beings. Pampering yourself time by time is essential for every single one of us. It teaches us how one should be taken care of and how to support each other.

3. You Have A Terrible Past Experience

This could be one of the reasons for your unapproachable nature towards people. When you keep some terrible memory or trauma stored inside of you, it's most likely you cannot comfort some other being. It won't seem like something you would do. Because you keep this emotional difference, you become distant and are forced to live with those memories, making things worse. It would help if you talked things out. Either your parents or your friends. Tell them whatever is on your mind, and you will feel light at heart. Nothing can change the past once it's gone, but we can work on the future.

4. You Got Heartbroken

In most cases, people are not born with this nature to be emotionally unavailable. It often comes with heartbreak. If you had a breakup with your partner, that could affect your emotional life significantly. And if it was a long-term relationship, then you got emotionally deprived. But on the plus side, you got single again. Ready to choose from scratch. Instead, you look towards all the negative points of this breakup. Who knows, maybe you'll find someone better.

5. You Are An Introvert

Do you hate going to parties or gatherings? Does meeting with friends sound tiresome? If yes, then surprise, you are an introvert. Social life can be a mess sometimes. Sometimes we prefer a book to a person. That trait of ours makes us emotionally unavailable for others. It is not a bad thing to stay at home on a Friday night, but going out once in a while may be healthy for you. And the easiest way to do that is to make an extrovert friend. Then you won't need to make an effort. Everything will go smoothly.

6. You Hate Asking For Help

Do you feel so independent that you hate asking for help from others? Sometimes when we get support from others, we feel like they did a favor for us. So, instead of asking for help, we prefer to do everything alone, by ourselves. Asking for aid, from superior or inferior, is no big deal. Everyone needs help sometimes.

Conclusion

Being emotionally unavailable doesn't make you a wrong person, but being there for others gives us self-comfort too. It's not all bad to interact with others; instead, it's pretty fun if you try. It will make your life much easier, and you will have a lot of support too.

Chapter 25:
Happy People Surround Themselves with The Right People

Whether we realized it or not, we become like the five people we spend the most time with. We start behaving like them, thinking like them, looking like them. We even make decisions based on what we think they would want us to do.

For example, there are many research findings that prove we are more likely to gain weight if a close friend or a family member becomes overweight. Similarly, we are more likely to engage in an exercise program if we surround ourselves with fit and health-oriented people.

So, who are the top 5 influencers in your life? Do they make you feel positive? Do they inspire and motivate you to be the best version of yourself? Do they support and encourage you to achieve your goals? Or, do they tell you that "it can't be done," "it's not possible," "you aren't good enough," "you will most likely fail."

If you feel emotionally drained by the energetic vampires in your life, you may want to detox your life and get rid of the relationships that aren't serving you in a positive way.

The negative people, the naysayers, the Debbie Downers, and the chronic complainers are like a dark cloud over your limitless potential.

They hold you back and discourage you from even trying because they're afraid that if you succeed, you'll prove them wrong.

Have the courage to remove the negative people from your life and watch how your energy and enthusiasm automatically blossom. Letting go of the relationships that aren't serving us is a critical step if we want to become more positive, fulfilled, and successful.

Detoxing your life from negative influencers will also allow you to become the person you truly want to be. You'll free yourself from constant judgment, negativity, and lack of support.

Here's what you can do:

- Stay away from chronic complainers.
- Stop participating in meaningless conversations.
- Share your ideas only with people who are supportive or willing to provide constructive criticism.
- Minimize your interactions with "friends," coworkers, and family members who are negative, discouraging, and bitter.
- Stop watching TV and reading negative posts on social media (yes, mainstream media is a major negative influence in our lives!).
- Surround yourself with positive and successful people (remember, we become like the top 5 people we spend our time with!).

- Find new, like-minded friends, join networking and support groups, or find a positive coach or a mentor.

If you want to make a positive change in your life, remember, the people around you have a critical influence on your energy, growth, and probability of success.

Positive people bring out the best in you and make you feel motivated and happy. They help you when you're in need, encourage you to go after your dreams, and are there to celebrate your successes or support you as you move past your challenges. Pick your top 5 wisely!

Chapter 26:

HOW A DAILY TO-DO LIST WILL CHANGE YOUR LIFE

To-do lists are generally underrated for a variety of reasons, and that's why we're giving you this article to go over some of the ways they can be useful to you as a professional, as well as a business owner. It's not likely that anyone within the sound of my voice has never used a to-do list at some point.

Meanwhile, many professionals don't regularly use them, depriving themselves of a simple tool that can help them be much more productive and keep everything in order. Here's why you need to start using lists.

It Helps You To Effectively Prioritize Tasks

When running a business, your day can quickly get away from you if you don't have it mapped out. With so many things that need attention, high volumes of customers, various requests throughout the day, and internal problems, you have to be an uncommonly organized type of person to keep track of all of it without writing it down.

And that's the whole point. It's not that you aren't capable of doing everything your job requires, it's just that you need a written reference to look at so that nothing is missed. When you've got a list for yourself to reference throughout the day, week, or even further, one important benefit of this is that it gives you the ability to lay out tasks in a specific order. That is, you can lay out the plan in an order from toughest to easiest, most time-consuming to least, or any other order that keeps your priorities straight.

It's mainly about making the best use of your time. Some things need to get done first due to deadlines, and some things need to be done at a specific time because they will take longer, which tasks will need a sufficient block of time that you might only have available at certain times of the day.

More Easily See The Progress Of Your Work

Part of the advantage of seeing your work progress is that you can perpetually learn if you need to reorder your priorities because if the more important work isn't getting done, then you probably need to move those jobs up on your list. Not only that but you may not have a full appreciation for just how satisfying it is to cross items off of a to-do list as you're performing your work, no matter what that work is.

This is especially true when you cross off the more challenging items. These to-do lists are just not valued nearly as much as they should be, which is probably a large part of the reason why people don't feel like it's all that important to use them. It's extremely good for a business owner, psychologically, to participate in physically crossing things off a to-do list, considering how stressful it can be when you're looking at everything you need to get done.

Naturally, this isn't much help to you if you don't get tasks done, so you can cross them off, which is good because it will motivate you more to complete tasks when you see all of them right in front of you.

Having a record of everything you've done, even down to a daily basis, is great for a reference because, in the future, you can look back at your records and see where you're at. Not only is it satisfying to see how much you've accomplished, but you'll also see where you're falling short and need to improve productivity.

Chapter 27:
8 Ways To Deal With Setbacks In Life

Life is never the same for anyone - It is an ever-changing phenomenon, making you go through all sorts of highs and lows. And as good times are an intrinsic part of your life, so are bad times. One day you might find yourself indebted by 3-digit figures while having only $40 in your savings account. Next day, you might be vacationing in Hawaii because you got a job that you like and pays $100,000 a year. There's absolutely no certainty to life (except passing away) and that's the beauty of it. You never know what is in store for you. But you have to keep living to see it for yourself. Setbacks in life cannot be avoided by anyone. Life will give you hardships, troubles, break ups, diabetes, unpaid bills, stuck toilet and so much more. It's all a part of your life.

Here's 8 ways that you might want to take notes of, for whenever you may find yourself in a difficult position in dealing with setback in life.

1. Accept and if possible, embrace it

The difference between accepting and embracing is that when you accept something, you only believe it to be, whether you agree or disagree. But when you embrace something, you truly KNOW it to be true and accept it as a whole. There is no dilemma or disagreement after you have embraced something.

So, when you find yourself in a difficult situation in life, accept it for what it is and make yourself whole-heartedly believe that this problem in your life, at this specific time, is a part of your life. This problem is what makes you complete. This problem is meant for you and only you can go through it. And you will. Period. There can be no other way.

The sooner you embrace your problem, the sooner you can fix it. Trying to bypass it will only add upon your headaches.

2. Learn from it

Seriously, I can't emphasize how important it is to LEARN from the setbacks you face in your life. Every hardship is a learning opportunity. The more you face challenges, the more you grow. Your capabilities expand with every issue you solve—every difficulty you go through, you rediscover yourself. And when you finally deal off with it, you are reborn. You are a new person with more wisdom and experience.

When you fail at something, try to explore why you failed. Be open-minded about scrutinizing yourself. Why couldn't you overcome a certain situation? Why do you think of this scenario as a 'setback'? The moment you find the answers to these questions is the moment you will have found the solution.

3. Execute What You Have Learnt

The only next step from here is to execute that solution and make sure that the next time you face a similar situation, you'll deal with it by having both your arms tied back and blindfolded. All you have to do is remember what you did in a similar past experience and reapply your previous solution.

Thomas A. Edison, the inventor of the light bulb, failed 10,000 times before finally making it. And he said "I have not failed. I just found 10,000 ways that won't work".

The lesson here is that you have to take every setback as a lesson, that's it.

4. Without shadow, you can never appreciate light

This metaphor is applicable to all things opposite in this universe. Everything has a reciprocal; without one, the other cannot exist. Just as without shadow, we wouldn't have known what light is, similarly, without light, we could've never known about shadow. The two opposites identify and complete each other.

Too much of philosophy class, but to sum it up, your problems in life, ironically, is exactly why you can enjoy your life. For example, if you are a chess player, then defeating other chess players will give you enjoyment while getting defeated will give you distress. But, when you are a chess prodigy—you have defeated every single chess player on earth and there's no one else to defeat, then what will you do to derive pleasure? Truth is, you can now no longer enjoy chess. You have no one to defeat. No one gives you the fear of losing anymore and as a result, the taste of winning has lost its appeal to you.

So, whenever you face a problem in life, appreciate it because without it, you can't enjoy the state of not having a problem. Problems give you the pleasure of learning from them and solving them.

5. View Every Obstacle As an opportunity

This one's especially for long term hindrances to your regular life. The COVID-19 pandemic for instance, has set us back for almost two years now. As distressing it is, there is also some positive impact of it. A long-term setback opens up a plethora of new avenues for you to explore. You suddenly get a large amount of time to experiment with things that you have never tried before.

When you have to pause a regular part of your life, you can do other things in the meantime. I believe that every one of us has a specific talent and most people never know what their talent is simply because they have never tried that thing.

6. Don't Be Afraid to experiment

People pursue their whole life for a job that they don't like and most of them never ever get good at it. As a result, their true talent gets buried under their own efforts. Life just carries on with unfound potential. But when some obstacle comes up and frees you from the clutches of doing what you have been doing for a long time, then you should get around and experiment. Who knows? You, a bored high school teacher, might be a natural at tennis. You won't know it unless you are fired from that job and actually play tennis to get over it. So whenever life gives you lemons, quit trying to hold on to it. Move on and try new things instead.

7. Stop Comparing yourself to others

The thing is, we humans are emotional beings. We become emotionally vulnerable when we are going through something that isn't supposed to be. And in such times, when we see other people doing fantastic things in life, it naturally makes us succumb to more self-loathing. We think lowly of our own selves and it is perfectly normal to feel this way. Talking and comapring ourselves to people who are seemingly untouched by setbacks is a counterproductive move. You will listen to their success-stories and get depressed—lose self-esteem. Even if they try their best to advise you, it won't get through to you. You won't be able to relate to them.

8. Talk to people other people who are having their own setbacks in life

I'm not asking you to talk to just any people. I'm being very specific here: talk to people who are going through bad times as well.

If you start talking to others who are struggling in life, perhaps more so compared to you, then you'll see that everyone else is also having difficulties in life. It will seem natural to you. Moreover, having talked with others might even show you that you are actually doing better than all these other people. You can always find someone who is dealing with more trouble than you and that will enlighten you. That will encourage you. If someone else can deal with tougher setbacks in life, why can't you?

Besides, listening to other people will give you a completely new perspective that you can use for yourself if you ever find yourself in a similar situation as others whom you have talked with.

Conclusion

Setbacks are a part of life. Without them we wouldn't know what the good times are. Without them we wouldn't appreciate the success that we have gotten. Without them we wouldn't cherish the moments that got us to where we are heading to. And without them there wouldn't be any challenge to fill our souls with passion and fire. Take setbacks as a natural process in the journey. Use it to fuel your drive. Use it to move your life forward one step at a time.

Chapter 28:
7 Ways to be More Mature in a Relationship

Intro:

Even if we love someone with all our heart, the reality of this life will be a reminder for us that nothing is ever as simple as it seems. You can ask anyone who has ever been in a relationship, and they will tell you that love is just one of the component you need for a committed relationship. But the important thing they will you that is essential for a relationship is maturity. Maturity is a skill that is not acquired from instinct and is instead learned. So, you might be wondering how one can act maturely in a relationship? Well, listen on, and you will get your answers.

1. Learn the values of respect, trust, and sincerity:

These are the essential ingredients of a healthy and happy relationship, and you should learn them as soon as you can. First, you need to trust your partner that they have the strength to fight for what you have. Second, you should appreciate their sincerity and also express genuine affection and love towards each other. Lastly, you should respect them as human being and as a person.

2. Address the needs of the relationship first:

When you are in a committed relationship, you are not thinking and making decisions for yourself and the other person, so there is no room for selfishness. Being mature in a relationship means working on your goals and making the right decisions that are beneficial for yourself and your partner. Whatever plans you have, they should be focused on the needs and wants of both of you because the consequences will affect not only your future but also theirs.

3. Accept the reality that people are not perfect:

When you get through your partner's bad moods and terrible tantrums and accept the worst parts of them, there is a huge chance that you guys are going to end up together. You have to accept the fact that the person you are in love with is not perfect; everyone has their flaws, and that is the beauty and complexity of a human, and once you accept that and see the beauty in them despite their flaws, that means you really love them, and that is also the mature move. However, you should always be aware that if they stoop too low, you should help them grow.

4. Practice patience and choose forgiveness:

The person you love can make you the happiest and at the same time break your heart in a million pieces. Love makes us vulnerable, and hence we get hurt easily. But you have to realize that just like you, your partner is only a human, and they can also make mistakes without realizing it. There can be moments when you will feel you are being taken for granted or that you have been betrayed, but you should not let these moments get to you. You should have patience, and that patience will give you strength, and when you forgive them, it will give you hope that everything is part of the process.

5. Relationships can't be perfect:

As we just mentioned, there will be days when the love of your life will break your heart or make you feel bad. And there are also going to be times when your wrong choices will affect your relationship or hurt your significant other. So, in those times, you should not lose hope and realize that no relationship is perfect and everything you are going through is just part of the process, and all the challenges you face will either make you or break you. But, you should be mature enough to not let them break you.

6. Recognize the power of words:

Words are extremely powerful; once you have said something, you can not take it back. Your words can make someone's day and can also make someone feel horrible about themselves. Therefore, you should make an active effort to learn what you should not express and what to say. Of course, you have the right to express whatever you are feeling, and it can be both good and bad, but you should never use this freedom to hurt the person you love the most.

7. Destructive consequences of overthinking:

One of the signs of maturity is to not let your destructive and damaging thoughts consume you. These destructive thoughts can ruin your relationship and even end it. Many younger couples do not have faith in their partners, which is the reason for their breakups, so it is important for mature adults to not act in the same way and let go of small things because, in the bigger picture, they will not matter.

Conclusion:

Life is difficult, and it takes a lot of time and maturity to figure it out and being in a relationship can make things complicated. So, even if you have lost someone because you were still figuring out things, you do not have to lose heart because you will soon find someone better.

Chapter 29:

Happy People Celebrate Other People's Success

What a phony smile... Why do people want him? How has he accomplished anything? It's ME they need. I'm the one who should be successful, not him. What a joke." This was my inner dialogue when I heard about other people's success. Like a prima donna, I seethed with jealousy and couldn't stand to hear about people doing better than me. But all the hating got me nowhere. So I thought about who I was really mad at...it wasn't the successful people I raged at. When I got more serious about succeeding, I channeled that useless envy into accepting myself.

I practiced self-acceptance with a journal, through affirmations, and by encouraging myself—especially when I failed. Then something weird happened. I started feeling happy for other people's success. Without a hint of irony, I congratulated people on their hard work, and I applauded their success with my best wishes. It felt good. I felt more successful doing it.

"Embrace your uniqueness. Time is much too short to be living someone else's life." – Kobi Yamada

My writing career caught fire at the same time. I was published on sites that I'd only dreamt of, and whose authors I had cussed for doing things that the egotistical me still hadn't. Congratulating others started a positive feedback loop. The more I accepted myself, the more I celebrated other people's success and the more I celebrated their success, the more success I achieved. Now that I look back, I could've hacked my growth curve by celebrating others' success as a daily ritual.

1. It conditions you for your own success

Feeling good for someone else's success helps you generate the same feelings you need for your own accomplishments. So put yourself in the other's shoes. Revel in their accomplishments; think of all the hard work that went into it. Celebrate their success and know that soon you'll experience the same thing for yourself. Apply the good feelings to your visions for a brighter future.

2. You'll transcend yourself

Everyone knows that to actually succeed, you need to be part of something bigger. But most people are kept from that bigger something by wanting all the focus for themselves. it's an ego issue.

Through celebrating others, you'll practice the selflessness it takes to let go of your tiny shell and leap into the ocean of success that comes through serving others. Cheer your fellow entrepreneurs. Feel their success. Let go of your want for recognition and accept that you'll get it when you help enough other people.

Chapter 30:
6 Signs You Have Found A Real Friend

Life seems easy when we have someone by our side. Everyone makes at least one friend in their life as if it comes naturally. That one person who we can rely on in difficult times. That one person who cares for us when we forget to care for ourselves. Friends are family that we get to choose ourselves. So, we have to decide that person exceptionally carefully. Friends are people who know who you are. You can share both joy and sadness with them without hesitating.

Friends have a significant impact on our lives. They can change us completely and help us shape ourselves into someone better. However, there might be some forgery in your way. Some people consider themselves as your friend, but we fail to notice that it is otherwise. So, it is imperative to choose a friend carefully, while an essential fraction is dependent on our friendship with someone. A good friend is the one whom you can count on to hold you when you require one. A friend is someone who becomes selfless when it comes to us. They always stay by your side as it said, "friends till the end."

1.You Can Be Yourself Around Them

No matter how you behave in front of your family or co-workers, you can always act like yourself in front of your friend. When they give you a sense of comfort, you automatically become yourself. That is the reason you never get tired of a friend. Because who gets tired of being who they are. A friend is a person who accepts us with all our flaws and stays by us even in our worst phase. They find beauty in your imperfections. That type of friend becomes necessary to keep around.

2. A Support For Good And Bad Times

We all are aware that support is what we want in our time of need. To share our difficult times and to share our good news with someone. A friend listens. They listen to whatever you want to ramble to them without complaining. They understand you and try to give to advice as well as possible. They are an excellent shoulder to cry on. They feel joy in your happiness. They feel sadness in your loss. Friends are people who love us, and thus, we give them ours in return.

3. You Trust Each Other

Trust is an essential foundation in any friendship. Otherwise, you are meant to fall apart. It would help if you grew that trust slowly. When you are loyal to each other, then there is nothing that comes between you two. You need to develop that trust slowly. When you are dedicated to each other, then there is nothing that comes between you two. Honesty is a must when it comes to building your trust with each other. If even one of you is lying about anything, then that friendship fails. Even if they didn't keep their promise, you can't trust them.

4. They Hype You Up

They won't fall back on complimenting you when you look your best. But a friend won't hesitate to confront you if you don't look good. That is what we like about them, and they won't make you look bad in front of others. They will make sure you know you are worth it. They will make you work for what you deserve. Friends will always try to hype you up and will accolade you. They know what you like and don't, so they shape you like you want to be shaped.

5.You Share Almost Everything

Two friends are always together in spirits. When something noteworthy happens in your life, you always feel the need to share it with someone. That someone will probably be a friend. You tend to share every little detail of any event of your life with them comfortably. They listen to you. And sometimes, they need to be listened to. That's where you come. You listen to them. Even the most intimate secrets are told sometimes. This exchanging of secrets can only be done when you feel safe sharing them with a person. A friend buries your secrets within themselves.

6. Good Memories

Even the most boring party can take a 360 degree turn when you are with your friend. Times like these call for good memories. It would help if you shared loads of good memories. Even when time passes by, a bad day can make an excellent future memory.

Conclusion

It takes a lot of time, care and love to form a strong bond of friendship. We have to give it our best to keep that bond in good condition. Friends are precious to us, and we should make them feel likewise. And with the right person, friendship can last a lifetime.

Chapter 31:

6 Ways To Get People To Like You

We are always trying for people to like us. We work on ourselves so that we can impress them. Everyone can not enjoy a single person. There will always be someone who dislikes them. But, that one person does not stop us from being charming and making people like us. In today's generation, good people are difficult to find. We all have our definition of being liked. We all have our type of person to select. That makes it very hard for someone to like someone by just knowing their name. We always judge people quickly, even to understand their nature. That makes it hard to like someone.

People always work their selves to be liked by the majority of people. It gives you a sense of comfort knowing that people are happy with you. You feel at ease when you know that people around you tend to smile by thinking about you. For that, you need to make an excellent first impression on people. Training yourself in such a way that you become everyone's favorite can sure be tiring. But, it always comes with a plus point.

1. Don't Judge

If you want people to like you, then you need to stop judging them. It is not good to consider someone based on rumors or by listening to one side of the story. Don't judge at all. We can never have an idea of what's going on in an individual life. We can not know what they are going through without them telling us. The best we can do is not judge them. Give them time to open up. Let them speak with you without the fear of being judged. Assuming someone is the worst without you them knowing is a horrendous thing to do.

2. Let Go of Your Ego and Arrogance

Make people feel like they can talk to you anytime they want. Arrogance will lead you nowhere. You will only be left alone in the end. So, make friends. Don't be picky about people. Try to get to know everyone with their own stories and theories. Make them feel comfortable around you to willingly come to talk to you and feel at ease after a few words with you. Being egotistic may make people fear you, but it will not make people like you. Be friendly with everyone around you.

3. Show Your Interest In People

When people talk about their lives, let them. Be interested in their lives, so it will make them feel unique around you. Make sure you listen attentively to their rant and remember as much as possible about a person. Even if they talk about something boring, try to make an effort towards them. If they talk about something worth knowledge, appreciate them. Ask them questions about it, or share your part of information with them, if you have any on that subject. Just try to make an effort, and people will like you instantly.

4. Try To Make New Friends

People admire others when they can click with anyone they meet. Making new friends can be a challenge, but it gives you confidence and, of course, new friends. Try to provide an excellent first impression and show them your best traits. Try to be yourself as much as possible, but do not go deep into friendship instantly. Give them time to adapt to your presence. You will notice that they will come to you themselves. That is because they like being around you. They trust you with their time, and you should valve it.

5. Be Positive

Everyone loves people. You give a bright, positive vibe. They tend to go to them, talk to them and listen to them. People who provide positive energy are easy to communicate with, and we can almost instantly become friends. Those are the type of people we can trust and enjoy being around. Positivity plays a critical role in your want to be liked. It may not be easy, but practice makes perfect. You have to give it your all and make everyone happy.

6. Be Physically and Mentally Present For The People Who Need You

People sometimes need support from their most trusted companion. You have to make sure you are there for them whenever they need you. Be there for them physically, and you can comfort someone without even speaking with them. Just hug them or just try to be there for them. It will make them feel peaceful by your presence. Or be there emotionally if they are ready. Try to talk to them. Listen to whatever they have to say, even if it doesn't make sense. And if they need comfort. Try to motivate them with your words.

Conclusion

You need to improve yourself immensely if you want people to like you. Make sure you do the right thing at the right time. Make people trust you and make them believe your words. Even a small gesture can make people like you. Have the courage to change yourself so that people will like you with all their heart's content.

CPSIA information can be obtained
at www.ICGtesting.com
Printed in the USA
BVHW032347201222
654656BV00010B/83